Masters of Music
THE WORLD'S GREATEST COMPOSERS

The Life and Times of

Antonio Lucio Vivaldi

Mitchell Lane
PUBLISHERS

P.O. Box 196
Hockessin, Delaware 19707

Masters of Music
THE WORLD'S GREATEST COMPOSERS

Titles in the Series
The Life and Times of...

Visit us on the web: www.mitchelllane.com

Comments? email us: mitchelllane@mitchelllane.com

Masters of Music
THE WORLD'S GREATEST COMPOSERS

The Life and Times of

Antonio Lucio Vivaldi

by Jim Whiting

Mitchell Lane
PUBLISHERS

Copyright © 2005 by Mitchell Lane Publishers, Inc. All rights reserved. No part of this book may be reproduced without written permission from the publisher. Printed and bound in the United States of America.

Printing   1   2   3   4   5   6   7   8

Library of Congress Cataloging-in-Publication Data
Whiting, Jim, 1943-
     Antonio Lucio Vivaldi/Jim Whiting.
          p. cm. — (Masters of music. World's greatest composers)
     Includes bibliographical references (p.) and index.
     Contents: Rediscovering a forgotten composer—The red priest—The Pietà—A burst of creative energy—The four seasons—In and out of fashion
          ISBN 1-58415-241-9 (lib bdg.)
     1. Vivaldi, Antonio, 1678-1741—Juvenile literature. 2. Composers—Italy—Biography—Juvenile literature. [1. Vivaldi, Antonio, 1648-1741. 2. Composers.] I. Title. II. Series.
ML3930.V58W44 2004
     780'.92—dc22   2003024044

ABOUT THE AUTHOR: Jim Whiting has been a journalist, writer, editor, and photographer for more than 20 years. In addition to a lengthy stint as publisher of *Northwest Runner* magazine, Mr. Whiting has contributed articles to the *Seattle Times*, *Conde Nast Traveler*, *Newsday*, and *Saturday Evening Post*. He has edited more than 20 titles in the Mitchell Lane Real-Life Reader Biography series and Unlocking the Secrets of Science. He lives in Washington state with his wife and two teenage sons.

PHOTO CREDITS: Cover: PhotoResearchers; p. 6 SuperStock; p.12 SuperStock; p. 15 SuperStock; p. 18 Corbis; p. 21 SuperStock; p. 24 PhotoResearchers; p. 32 Corbis; p. 38 Hulton/Archive

PUBLISHER'S NOTE: This story is based on the author's extensive research, which he believes to be accurate. Documentation of such research is contained on page 47.

The internet sites referenced herein were active as of the publication date. Due to the fleeting nature of some web sites, we cannot guarantee they will all be active when you are reading this book.

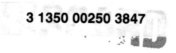

Contents

The Life and Times of
Antonio Lucio Vivaldi

by Jim Whiting

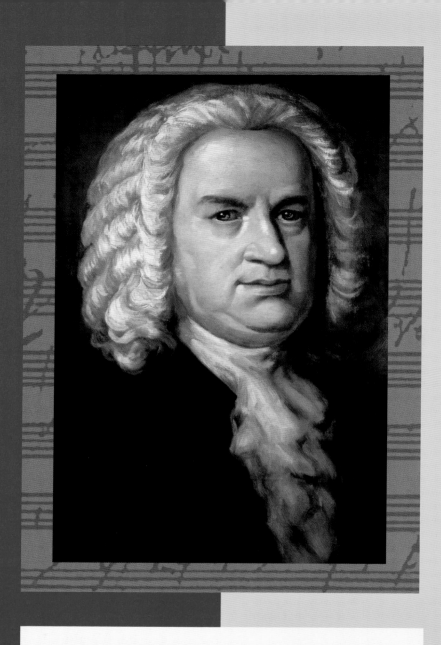

After Johann Sebastian Bach, pictured here, died in 1750, his works were nearly forgotten. Composer Felix Mendelssohn led a performance of Bach's St. Matthew Passion in 1829. That led to a revival of interest in Bach's other compositions, which in turn led to a rediscovery of Vivaldi's work as well. Yet it would take many years before his work would be fully appreciated.

Rediscovering a Forgotten Composer

I n 1999, a British magazine called *The Radio Times* conducted a poll among its readers to determine their favorite piece of classical music. Many people were surprised at the results. The winner wasn't something by Beethoven, such as his famous Fifth or Ninth (Choral) Symphony. Nor was it one of the beloved pieces played at Christmas, George Frideric Handel's *Messiah* or Peter Tchaikovsky's *Nutcracker.* Even though many musicians consider Johann Sebastian Bach to be history's greatest composer, the winner wasn't one of his works either.

The readers' favorite was *The Four Seasons* by Italian composer Antonio Vivaldi.

If that poll had been conducted 50 years earlier, the results would have been different, and not because people's musical tastes had changed. There was another reason.

Until 1950, hardly anyone had heard of either Vivaldi or his music. Unlike many other famous composers, Vivaldi was forgotten almost as soon as he died in 1741, alone and far from home. His body was hurriedly thrown into an unmarked grave, and his music seemed to suffer the same fate.

Vivaldi wrote what is called Baroque music, which is very grandiose. One characteristic of Baroque music is that several melodic lines wind around each other. Another is that there are many dramatic contrasts, such as alternating loud and soft passages. Perhaps most important, the music features a great deal of ornamentation. Baroque singers commonly stretch out a simple phrase for a minute or two, often repeating one or more words in the phrase.

Vivaldi had been very popular while he was alive, but time seemed to have passed him by. His music had fallen out of fashion. Melodic lines became simpler, and there was very little ornamentation.

His return to fame came by a curious route. Less than 10 years following Vivaldi's death, Bach died. Most people believed that several of Bach's sons, who had become composers like their father, were much better and more interesting than whoever had come before.

But unlike what happened with Vivaldi, a handful of admirers kept Bach's reputation and music alive during the following decades. Early in the 1820s, a young German composer named Felix Mendelssohn found a copy of Bach's *St. Matthew Passion.* Astonished by its beauty, he immediately wanted to present it in public. Despite several obstacles, he stubbornly pushed forward with his dream and conducted a performance in 1829.

The concert was an overwhelming success. Suddenly Bach was back in favor. People began demanding to hear his other works. Musicians searched frantically for manuscripts he had written. It was a complicated process, because these manuscripts had been scattered far and wide.

All this searching eventually turned up a collection known as *XII Concerti di Vivaldi elaborati di J.S. Bach* ("12 concertos of Vivaldi

transcribed by J.S. Bach"). Soon some of Vivaldi's other works that had also influenced Bach were discovered. "Who is this Vivaldi?" people asked.

As Vivaldi biographer Marc Pincherle observes, "We are reminded of the Egyptologists who, digging in the Valley of the Kings in search of a certain pharaoh's burial place, uncover an older, hitherto unsuspected tomb."[1]

But Vivaldi's music wasn't destined to become an overnight success. Its eventual revival has some elements of a detective story.

This story began with a nobleman from Genoa named Count Giacomo Durazzo, who was very interested in music. He spent a great deal of time in Vienna, then was appointed by Austrian Empress Maria Theresa as ambassador to Venice in 1775. While Durazzo was serving in Venice, he accumulated a huge collection of Vivaldi's music. After his death in 1794, the collection disappeared.

Part of it turned up in 1926 in the possession of a monastery that had to raise money to carry out repairs. The monastery called on Alberto Gentili, a music professor at the University of Turin in Italy, to determine its value. Gentili also helped find a buyer.

It was obvious to Gentili that there was another portion of music somewhere. He researched the history of the Durazzo family and tracked down the original count's last surviving descendant, Marchese Giuseppe Durazzo. At first the old man refused to let Gentili examine his library to see if it even contained any Vivaldi manuscripts. Finally he gave permission, and Gentili found what he was looking for. Once again, he was able to find a buyer, but the Marchese demanded that the music never be published or performed. Gentili and others went to court and the ban was finally lifted.

Soon afterward, in 1939, Antonio Vivaldi's music was performed in public for the first time in nearly 200 years. That was the eve of World War II, and nothing further happened for several years. Soon after the war ended, however, the famous music publishing house of G. Ricordi in Milan, Italy, began distributing Vivaldi's instrumental works.

In 1950, Ricordi published *The Four Seasons.* Later that year, Italian record company Cetra issued the first recording of the music. It created a sensation.

H. C. Robbins Landon writes, "In 1950, I happened to be in New York when the famous Cetra recording of *The Four Seasons* arrived at the Liberty Music Shop and a clerk put it on. The shoppers, myself included, stopped their own activities and started to listen, entranced, to his seductive music which had lain forgotten on library shelves for two hundred years.

"The Vivaldi renaissance had begun. It was to continue until, in 1990, Nigel Kennedy's recording of *The Four Seasons* topped the bestseller lists in London for many months. *The Four Seasons,* in short, has become the most popular piece of classical music in the world."[2] ◆

Two Baroque Masters

Bach

Johann Sebastian Bach and George Frideric Handel are the two other great composers of the Baroque era. Though they were born in Germany within a month of each other in 1685, they never met.

Handel

Bach came from the most famous musical family of all time. At least 40 of his ancestors and descendants were musicians, and he naturally learned how to play several instruments as a child. He became especially skilled as an organ player, and during his lifetime he was more famous as an organist than as a composer.

He married his cousin Maria Barbara Bach when he was about 21. She died suddenly in 1720, and soon afterward he married a singer named Anna Magdalena Wilcke. Between his two wives he had 20 children, though 10 died in infancy or early childhood.

Bach had several jobs when he was a young man, then spent the last 27 years of his life in the city of Leipzig. Though he was practically ignored after his death in 1750, many people now regard him as the greatest composer of all time. *Voyager 1* and *2,* spacecraft launched in 1977, carry a gold-plated vinyl record with many types of information so that any beings deep in space might learn something about us. Part of the record contains music. Of the 27 selections, 3 are Bach's.

Handel, who was born to a nonmusical family, became a musician despite his father's objections. Unlike Bach, who lived his entire life in Germany, Handel traveled extensively. Eventually he settled in England and became a British subject. He was famous both as a composer and a promoter of operas and concerts. As a result, he made much more money than Bach ever earned. Unlike Bach, Handel never married. He died in 1759.

Today Handel is most remembered for his *Messiah,* which he composed in 1741. It is still performed in thousands of concerts every year at Christmas.

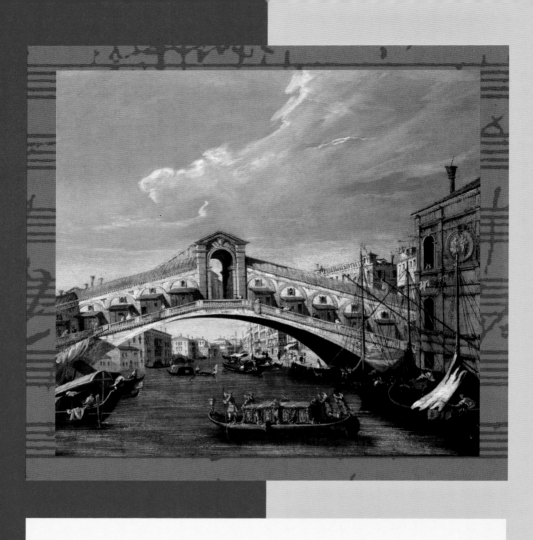

This view of the Rialto Bridge in Venice, Italy was painted by the Italian artist, Giovanni Antonio Canaletto during Vivaldi's lifetime. Vivaldi spent most of his life in Italy, although he died in Vienna, Austria.

CHAPTER 2

The Red Priest

T he earliest records of anyone named Vivaldi are of two brothers from Genoa, Italy. They were seamen who apparently helped discover the Canary Islands off the western coast of Africa in 1291. Almost exactly two centuries later, a much more famous Genoese seaman named Christopher Columbus would use those islands as his final point of departure before his voyage that resulted in the discovery of the New World.

Antonio Vivaldi's more immediate ancestors were content with less adventurous pursuits. In 1665, at the age of 10, his father, Giovanni Battista Vivaldi, moved from the family home of Brescia, Italy, to Venice with his widowed mother. By the time he became an adult, he was making a living as a barber. Perhaps his bright red hair—very unusual in Italians—was the reason for his interest in this occupation. He was also a skilled musician who played the violin. Eventually Giovanni devoted himself entirely to music. He became good enough to join the orchestra of San Marco (St. Mark's), one of the city's best, in 1685.

He also devoted himself to Camilla Calicchio, the daughter of a tailor. They were married on August 6, 1677. Antonio Lucio Vivaldi, their first child, was born on March 4 the following year. Because of what may have been a premature birth, he was a weak infant. His church's baptismal register records that *per pericolo di morte* ("on account of the risk of death"), he had to be baptized right away by the midwife who delivered him.

It is likely that even from birth he was affected by a chest condition that was to bother him for much of his life. While no one knows the exact nature of the ailment, the most common theory is that it was a severe case of asthma. Whatever the problem, the infant needed two months to become strong enough to be taken to the church for his formal baptism. Eventually Antonio would be joined by at least five other brothers and sisters, though he was the only one who followed in Giovanni's footsteps as a musician.

We know almost nothing of Antonio's childhood and education. The family home was located near the Arsenal, the main shipyard in Venice. But despite the occupations of his early ancestors and the importance of the sea to Venice—every year there was an immense parade that concluded with the doge (the city's elected ruler) throwing a consecrated ring into the water to symbolize Venice's "marriage" with the surrounding ocean—Antonio wasn't interested in becoming a sailor. From an early age, he probably was influenced by his father's musical skill. It is very likely that he learned to play the violin from his father. There are some reports that he was skilled enough to play occasionally in the cathedral orchestra by the time he was 10.

Despite his early interest in music and the ability that he quickly developed, Antonio began training to become a priest when he was 15. Because of his father's occupation as a cathedral musician—as well as his own possible involvement with the orchestra—he would have come into frequent contact with church officials. At that time, it wasn't uncommon for clergymen to be also actively

involved in music. There was probably another reason for choosing the priesthood as well. Since Antonio came from humble origins, becoming a priest would have improved his social status.

The first step toward his vocation came on September 18, 1693, when he received the tonsure. That is a special haircut in which the top of the head is shaved. For Antonio, this would have left a nar-

The Church of the Blessed Sacrament in Venice was painted by Canaletto in the early 18th century. Today, this painting hangs in the Louvre, in Paris, France.

row fringe of the bright red hair, which he had inherited from his father, encircling his skull. He received the first of the four minor orders en route to the priesthood the following day when he became an *ostario* (porter). He was named a *lettore* (lector) on September 21, 1694, followed by *esorcista* (exorcist) on December 25, 1695, and *accolito* (acolyte) on September 21, 1696. He moved into the higher orders when he became a *suddiacone* (subdeacon) on April 4, 1699, and *diacone* (deacon) on September 18, 1700. He was finally ordained as a priest on March 12, 1703.

Ten years is an unusually long period of training for the priesthood. Vivaldi's health might have been one reason for the delay. Another may have been that he didn't enter a seminary. Apparently continued to live at home, serving as an assistant under the supervision of the priests at several nearby churches. A third, even more likely reason is that he continued to study music during this entire period. By this time those studies would have broadened to include musical composition as well as playing the violin.

Though it may have taken him a long time to achieve ordination, becoming a priest provided Antonio with the nickname that he would bear for the rest of his life: *il prete rosso,* or the Red Priest. But the priesthood would not provide him with a long career.

The City of Flooded Streets

Venice, Italy, is one of the world's most famous cities. Millions of tourists visit every year. Arriving by train, they step out of the railroad station onto a broad plaza. At the edge of the plaza is the Grand Canal. It is the largest of the hundreds of waterways in the city that serve as roads. There are no automobiles in Venice.

Grand Canal, Venice

According to tradition, the city was founded on March 25, 421, by Romans and other people from the mainland of Italy who were fleeing barbarian invasions. They settled on a group of small islands in a lagoon that was protected from the open sea. There they established a republic headed by an elected ruler known as a doge. The islands were eventually linked by a series of bridges, and much of the lagoon was filled in with dirt. Hundreds of gondolas, long narrow boats painted black and propelled by an oarsman standing at the rear, ferried people from place to place.

Over the next millennium, the city's importance gradually increased. By the middle of the 15th century, Venice was the greatest naval power in Europe. Its Arsenal, or shipyard, employed more than 15,000 people. It was said that a new Venetian ship was launched every day. These ships helped protect the trade routes throughout the Mediterranean Sea. In addition to the mainland city of Constantinople (which is now Istanbul, Turkey), the Venetian Empire included the islands of Crete (now part of Greece) and Cyprus (a republic just south of Turkey).

The rise of the Muslim Ottoman Empire in Turkey presented a threat to Venice. After the Turks recaptured Constantinople in 1453, Venetian power gradually lessened over the course of the next few centuries. The city lost its independence in 1797 when an army of Napoléon entered it.

Today, speedboats and larger boats called *vaporetti,* the main form of public transportation, have largely replaced the gondola. However, the sleek black boats still have their place as tourists hire them for short excursions through the wondrous waterways.

This engraved portrait of Antonio Vivaldi shows him holding a partially written composition.

The Pietà

66 Barely ordained a priest," Antonio Vivaldi explained in a letter he wrote many years later, "I said Mass for a year or a little longer, and then I abandoned it, having had to leave the altar three times because of the same complaint."[1] Almost certainly this "same complaint" was the chest ailment that he may have suffered at birth and that would plague him for the rest of his life. The amount of speaking and chanting he needed to do to perform his priestly duties would have placed great demands on his lungs. Asthma, if that was indeed the disease from which he suffered, would have often made it hard for him to breathe normally, let alone project his voice to the farthest corners of a large church.

According to another story, "Once, while reading daily mass, he was overcome by the urge to compose. He interrupted his priestly functions and went into the sacristy to discharge his musical thoughts and then returned to end the ceremony. Of course, the matter immediately created a stir and Vivaldi was brought before the church authorities for disciplinary action. The body in question was lenient and decided to relieve him of the duty of celebrating mass in the future, since it appeared that he was not quite right in the head."[2]

His problems fulfilling the obligations expected of him as a priest didn't extend to his musicianship. Within six months after his ordination, he was hired as *maestro di violino* (violin teacher) at the Seminario Musicale dell'Ospedale della Pietà. He would stay with this establishment for much of the rest of his life.

The Pietà was one of several similar institutions in Venice. They were orphanages that carried the name *ospedale* (hospital) because they had originally been attached to infirmaries. The first ones had been founded in the 14th century to care for what was a growing problem of homeless children in the city. Eventually they were limited to girls. Their primary purpose was to give the girls a secure home and provide them with a basic education.

But they soon went well beyond that purpose. Even before Vivaldi's time, some of the girls received a primarily musical education. They were known as *figlie di coro*, or "girls of the chorus," though the term *chorus* also included the members of the orchestra. Four of the *ospedali*, including the Pietà, gained a great deal of renown for the quality of their musical presentations.

With Venice's power and influence somewhat in decline, it was expensive to maintain these *ospedali*, which often contained in excess of a thousand girls. To help raise money, they gave frequent public concerts. Not surprisingly, there was a great deal of competition among the four. They were concerned about making sure that the performances met the highest standards. These concerts appealed not just to Venetians but also to tourists, in much the same way that people today might attend a musical concert as part of a tour to a famous city.

The comments made by a visitor named Charles de Brosses were typical of many about the quality of the performances: "They [the girls] sing like angels and play the violin, flute, the organ, the

oboe, the cello and the bassoon; in short there is no instrument, however unwieldy, that can frighten them. The one of the four Ospedali I visit most often, and where I enjoy myself most, is the Ospedale della Pietà; it is also the first for the perfection of the symphonies."[3]

One reason for the excellence of the performances was that the "girls" were often young or even middle-aged women with years of musical training and performances behind them. At that time, there were few professional musical opportunities for women. Orchestras were limited to men. Many women musicians continued to live in the same place where they had grown up.

The Pietà, like the other *ospedali,* was under the control of a board of governors, nearly all of them upper-class citizens of

The Molo, Venice, painted around 1735 by Italian artist Giovanni Canaletto. This painting hangs in the Kimball Art Museum in Fort Worth, Texas.

Venice. They kept careful records, which provide us with a great deal of what we know about Vivaldi.

These records indicate that Antonio Vivaldi was hired in September 1703 at an annual salary of 60 ducats. At that time he was 25 years old. Within a year, Vivaldi's work was appreciated so much that he received a pay increase to 100 ducats a year, a raise of nearly 70 percent. Vivaldi's work with the Pietà had another benefit besides the money he earned. He had what was practically a personal orchestra to work with. He could try out his musical ideas with a talented group of dedicated musicians. It is not surprising that his first published work, a collection of trio sonatas, appeared in 1705, less than two years after he began at the Pietà.

But all was not well. Though his contract was renewed each year, the margin of approval grew steadily narrower.

Finally the unthinkable happened.

Antonio Vivaldi was fired. ◆

WORLD'S MOST FAMOUS VIOLINS

With modern advances in technology, just about everything we use represents a big improvement from the time of its invention. DVDs and CDs reproduce music far more faithfully than the first records for record players, which were made more than a century ago. Today's televisions are far superior to the first boxy, bulky black-and-white sets that appeared during the 1940s. And even the lowest-priced modern automobile gives far better performance and goes much faster than Henry Ford's Model T, introduced in 1908.

Antonio Stradivari

But there is one exception: when it comes to violins, nothing gives a better tone than the instruments that Antonio Stradivari made nearly 300 years ago. About 600 are still in existence. It's not uncommon for "Strads," as they are affectionately called by symphony musicians, to be worth millions of dollars.

Most musicians can't afford to pay that kind of money. But sometimes they have the opportunity to play a Stradivarius for a few hours or even days. They approach the experience with the same reverence that a baseball player might take to stepping up to the plate with a bat that Babe Ruth or Joe DiMaggio once used.

Stradivari (1644–1737) was from Cremona, a town in northern Italy about 25 miles southeast of Milan. He probably learned his trade from the Amati family, who, along with the Guarneris, produced violins that are almost as well regarded as Strads. But Stradivari didn't leave behind anything written that might shed light on his exact construction methods. Violin makers today can duplicate just about everything about a Strad: the shape, the type of wood, the varnish. But they can't duplicate the tone.

Several theories have tried to explain why Strads have such a unique tone. One is that Stradivari put a thin layer of volcanic ash called pozzolana between the varnish and the wood. Another is that a slimy fungus growing on the wood destroyed enzymes that changed its texture and therefore its tone. But no one knows for sure.

This portrait of Antonio Vivaldi was painted in the 18th century by Francois Morellon La Cave. It currently hangs in the Museum of Music in Bologna, Italy.

A Burst of Creative Energy

No one is exactly sure why Vivaldi was fired from the Pietà. Unfortunately, the records of the Pietà reveal nothing about the reason. It certainly didn't have anything to do with the way he did his job. As Walter Kolneder says, "The fact that soon [after Vivaldi was hired] the Ospedale della Pietà outshone the other institutions with its outstanding orchestra can doubtless be ascribed to the particular merits of Vivaldi."[1] Perhaps his initial successes created jealous enemies. He may have been a difficult man to work with. There is another theory. Vivaldi may have been such a good instructor that he literally taught himself out of a job.

Shortly after Vivaldi was fired, German composer George Frideric Handel visited Venice and presented his new opera, *Agrippina*. It had 17 performances, an especially long run at that time. We don't know if the two men met, but it is highly likely that they did. And there can be little doubt that the performance of the opera had a great influence on Vivaldi.

The Venetians loved opera. The world's first opera house was built there in 1637, and from that point on composers vied with each other to produce exciting special effects. They had to, because

the audiences behaved much differently than they do now. By modern standards, they were very rude. They talked during the performance, ate, drank, and gambled. One foreign visitor even reported that a big gob of spit landed on the libretto that he was reading as he was trying to follow along.

There is little news of Vivaldi for two years, then just as mysteriously as he had been fired, he was rehired in 1711. This time the vote was unanimous.

"Realizing the necessity of securing ever better instrumental tuition for the girls studying music in order to increase the reputation of this pious establishment, the post of violin master being vacant, we move that Don Antonio Vivaldi be appointed violin master at an annual salary of 60 ducats, this governing body being certain that he will exercise his talent to the utmost in the good service of this pious establishment, and for the greater profit of those girls," the governors wrote.[2]

That same year also marked the publication of one of his most famous compositions, *L'estro armonico,* a series of 12 concertos for varying groups of instruments. It would become one of the most influential pieces of music published during that time.

Publication of *L'estro armonico* demonstrated his mastery of a relatively new musical form, the concerto. It would remain one of his signature forms during his entire career. In a concerto, a solo instrument alternates with the orchestra. It almost always has three movements. The first movement is usually fast, the second is slower, and the third is once again fast.

"Vivaldi is best known as a composer of concertos," according to author John Booth. "Not surprisingly, most have the violin as the solo instrument. The principal emphasis of the Vivaldian type of

solo concerto is its emphasis on the freedom of the individual instrument, a freedom which clearly appealed to Vivaldi the virtuoso, enabling him to display the full range of his talent."[3]

In 1713, the Pietà's chief composer, Francesco Gasparini, had to leave because of illness. Vivaldi was asked to begin writing sacred music, a new form for him. He had to write masses, motets, vespers, and other types. Satisfying this new demand illustrates his ability to compose rapidly.

With the sensation caused by *Agrippina* still fresh in his mind, the versatile Vivaldi somehow found time to write his first opera, *Ottone in villa*, in 1713. Perhaps feeling a little unsure of himself, he took it to the nearby town of Vicenza. It was very successful.

In 1714, he wrote another group of violin concertos, called *La stravaganza* (The Extravagance). Venetian audiences were looking for bigger and better entertainments, and Vivaldi knew how to create them.

He also wrote his second opera, *Orlando finto pazzo,* that year, and presented it in Venice. He soon realized that as the composer, he didn't have much say in the way his work was presented. People came to operas to hear their favorite singers perform. Sometimes the singers would change the music.

So Vivaldi became an impresario. That meant he was in charge of the entire production. First he had to compose the opera. While that may seem like a full-time job in itself, he claimed that he composed one of his operas in just five days. Then when it was finished, he had to do everything from selling tickets to hiring the singers and supervising the rehearsals.

All this talent didn't go unnoticed. A German nobleman named Johann Friedrich von Uffenbach, who visited Venice in 1715, wrote,

"After supper I received a visit from Vivaldi, the famous composer and violinist, having several times sent an invitation to his house when discussing some concerti grossi which I wished to order from him, and also having a few bottles of wine fetched for him, knowing that he was a cleric. He let me listen to his very difficult and quite inimitable [matchless] fantasias on the violin, so that, being close at hand, I could not but marvel at his skill."[4]

Three days later Vivaldi appeared with the 10 concerti grossi that von Uffenbach had ordered. While some people don't believe that Vivaldi could have composed them that quickly, Charles de Brosses wrote that Vivaldi "composes furiously and prodigiously. I have heard him undertake to compose a concerto with all its parts more quickly than a copyist could copy it."[5]

All these successes still did not seem to impress Vivaldi's employers, the governors of the Pietà. Early in 1716, he almost lost his job again. Twice he didn't get the two-thirds vote he needed to continue. Finally a couple of the governors switched their votes and the contract was renewed.

He quickly rewarded them by overseeing his biggest production for the girls to date. That summer, Venice defeated Turkey in a battle at the island of Corfu. As a patriotic Venetian, Vivaldi wrote an oratorio to celebrate the victory.

An oratorio is similar to an opera, with music for chorus and solos, but there is no staging or acting. The subjects often come from the Bible. Vivaldi had already written one in 1714. It was called *Moyses deus Pharaonis* and dealt with Moses and the Egyptian pharaoh.

For this new oratorio, he chose the Old Testament story of Judith and Holofernes and named it *Juditha triumphans*. In the story, Holofernes is a general sent by the Babylonian king

Nebuchadrezzar to put down a rebellion of Jews around 588 B.C. Judith, a beautiful Jewish widow, appeals for mercy for her town. Holofernes invites her to his tent but soon falls asleep. Judith beheads him, and the act saves her town from destruction.

In his oratorio, Vivaldi saw the victory over the Turks as giving a similar result to Venice. The city, like Judith's town, was saved. The victory might even help restore the city to the glory it had enjoyed earlier. The combination of patriotic excitement and Vivaldi's excellent music made *Juditha triumphans* an enormous success when it was first presented late in 1716. Even now it is considered to be one of his masterpieces.

Up to this point, Vivaldi had lived in the same city for virtually his entire life. Beginning in 1718, he spent three or four years away from Venice. He was hired at the court of Prince Philip of Darmstadt at Mantua, a city about 100 miles from Venice. While it was close enough for him to return to Venice occasionally, the records of the governors of the Pietà contain nothing about Vivaldi for four years.

At Mantua, Vivaldi continued writing operas, and soon his fame began to spread even wider. He wrote operas for cities such as Florence and Munich, and he often traveled to them to make sure the operas were performed the way he wanted them to be done.

He reappears in the Pietà records in 1723, but it is obvious that things had changed. By then he had become famous all over Europe. He was no longer serving as a teacher. Under the terms of his new contract, his obligation was simply to produce two concerts of his own works each month, which would also include several rehearsals. In today's terms, he would be considered almost as a freelance composer.

He made three trips to Rome to present his operas there. Audiences also thronged to his concerts to hear him play the violin. The highlight came in 1724 when he was asked to play at the Vatican for Pope Innocent XIII. Because Vivaldi was a priest, he must have felt especially honored.

In 1725, he was asked to write a Gloria for the wedding ceremonies of the French king Louis XV, evidence of how far his reputation had spread. That was also the year he would publish the music that eventually propelled him to the top of the classical music charts. ◆

THE SUN KING

Louis XIV was the king of France for 72 years, the longest reign of any European monarch in history. His rule lasted so long that his successor was his great-grandson, who became Louis XV.

But this long reign almost never happened. His father, King Louis XIII, hated his wife Anne and tried to avoid her as much as he could. They were married for 23 years before Louis, their first child, was born in 1638. When he was just four, his father died of tuberculosis and the little boy became Louis XIV. Because he was so young, his mother Anne ruled France with the aid of Cardinal Jules Mazarin.

Louis XIV

As a teenager, Louis fell in love with Marie Mancini, the Cardinal's niece. But royal marriages were usually made for political reasons. Louis had to marry Maria Theresa, the daughter of the king of Spain.

Cardinal Mazarin died in 1661 and Louis XIV was finally able to rule in his own name. Later he made a famous statement, "I am the state," meaning he considered himself to be an absolute monarch. He also called himself the Sun King as a way of showing how important he regarded himself. While he was king, France became one of the most important world powers. Louis XIV also encouraged the growth of the arts.

Louis XIV is most famous for building the royal palace at Versailles, several miles outside Paris. He erected many elaborate buildings. One housed the Hall of Mirrors, nearly as long as a football field and lined with huge mirrors. The extensive grounds enclosed a garden, lake, zoo, hundreds of fountains, and a vast hunting park. By the end of Louis's reign in 1715, the total area at Versailles was 23 square miles, the size of many large cities today, and 10,000 people lived there.

The palace was damaged during the French Revolution in 1789, but it has been restored and is one of France's most popular tourist sites.

Court de Marbre at the Palace of Versailles

This portrait of Ludwig van Beethoven is by an unknown artist. It now hangs in the Gesellschaft der Musikfreunde (Society of the Friends of Music) in Vienna, Austria. There is evidence in Beethoven's music that he was influenced by Vivaldi's compositions.

Masters of Music

CHAPTER 5

The Four Seasons

The Four Seasons (in Italian, *Le quatro stagioni*) may be the world's favorite work of classical music. Technically, however, there is no such composition. Rather, what we call *The Four Seasons* is part of Vivaldi's *Il cimento dell'armonia e dell'inventione* (The Contest Between Harmony and Invention). The entire composition contains 12 concertos, of which *The Four Seasons* are the first four. It is likely that Vivaldi had himself in mind when he wrote it, because the solo violin is the instrument that is most often featured. These passages allowed him to show off his extraordinary ability.

The Four Seasons is the first example of what we call program music, in which the music is meant to convey a certain impression. Vivaldi began the printed score with four sonnets—a particular type of poem that contains 14 lines—that he probably wrote himself. Each poem describes specific images that correspond with the season. Some of these are natural: birds singing, the heat of the sun, a brief but violent thunderstorm. Others show human activities: dancing, drinking, hunting, even sleeping. The music carefully follows the words of the sonnets. Frequent notes in the score contain specific instructions for the musicians.

33

La primavera (Spring) is the first of the four concertos. It opens with various instruments imitating the singing of birds. Then the surface of a small brook is ruffled by a gentle breeze. Suddenly a storm springs up and the music becomes more agitated. Soon it passes and the birds return to their nests. The scene shifts to a shepherd asleep, his dog at his side. The dog is wide awake and a viola vividly re-creates its barking and howling. The concerto ends with a peasant dance.

L'estate (Summer) follows. It begins with a musical depiction of summer's stifling heat. Several birds begin singing. Again a storm breaks out. A shepherd tries to rest after it passes, but flies and hornets buzzing nearby won't give him any peace. Then the storm returns, even more violently, cutting down corn and other crops.

These violent storms are only a distant memory as *L'autunno (Autumn)* celebrates harvest time with country dancing and drunken shepherds. One of them—represented by a solo violin—breaks up the rhythm of the dancers. If you listen carefully to the music, you can even hear him hiccuping. After a passage marked *ubriachi dormienti* ("sleeping drunks"), the disruption ends and the dancing goes on. The concerto continues with a hunt. The prey tries to escape, but it can't elude the hunters' guns and the pursuing dogs that are barking excitedly. The wounded animal makes a final feeble attempt at freedom, but it gasps and dies.

The final concerto, *L'inverno (Winter)*, demonstrates musically how cold Venice can become in the winter when chilly winds sweep over the lagoon. People tremble and stamp their feet, and Vivaldi uses a special technique in the solo violin part to imitate the sound of chattering teeth. The cold is quickly forgotten in the middle section as people sit comfortably by the fire while the rain beats down outside. Back outside once again, they walk carefully on thin ice, sometimes slipping musically and tumbling to the frozen

ground. Then the winds begin to howl again, so the last line of Vivaldi's poem is not entirely convincing, since it reads, "This is winter, but it brings joy."

As Robbins Landon observes, "*The Four Seasons* has certainly brought joy to what is now quite literally millions of people all over the civilized world—a situation which would certainly have astonished Vivaldi, who considered himself in many ways to be a modest cog in the universe."[1]

And it isn't just our era that has been affected. The work enjoyed immediate popularity as soon as it was published. It became a special favorite of Louis XV, but its appeal wasn't limited to royalty. It influenced composers for nearly 100 years. Ludwig van Beethoven's Sixth (Pastoral) Symphony, composed in 1808, includes many of the same images that Vivaldi used: shimmering country brooks, shepherds dancing, a violent thunderstorm. Many violinists of Vivaldi's era considered *The Four Seasons* to be a vital part of their repertoire. There is evidence that at least one musician was still playing it more than 50 years after Vivaldi's death. ◆

This map of Europe shows some of the places that Vivaldi visited in his lifetime. He played the violin for Pope Innocent XIII during a 1724 visit to Rome. He traveled to Munich, Prague and Vienna during the late 1720s and early 1730s to produce his operas there. His final trip was to Vienna late in 1740. He died there the following year.

The Dodo

Sometimes people may insult other people by calling them a "dodo bird" or "as dumb as a dodo." The dodo was a flightless bird that became one of the first species to become extinct because of contact with human beings. But this extinction probably didn't have anything to do with how smart or stupid the bird may have been.

Millions of years ago the ancestors of the dodo, birds similar to modern pigeons, landed on Mauritius. This small, isolated island is in the southern Indian Ocean far off the eastern coast of Africa.

According to one theory, over a period of many years the dodos lost the ability to fly. They didn't need to fly, because there were no predators from which the birds needed to escape and there was plenty of fruit lying on the ground. Gradually the birds grew larger. Eventually they became perfectly adapted to their environment.

Portuguese sailors discovered Mauritius early in the 16th century. They used the island as a source of fresh food, stopping there after enduring voyages of many months. The dodos were easy prey.

The birds probably could have survived occasional visits from hungry seafarers, but Dutch colonists began settling on the island in 1598. They too hunted the birds for food. But what doomed the dodos was what the settlers brought with them: pigs, monkeys, dogs, cats, and rats. Dodos nested on the ground. As the settlers cut down the forests to make room for themselves, these nests were left out in the open. The newly introduced animals ate the eggs and the young birds that managed to hatch.

A few live birds were taken to Europe, where artists made paintings of them. Those paintings give us some idea of what the birds looked like. As the number of dodos declined, no one tried to save them.

The last known dodo was seen in 1680 or 1681. A species that had lived successfully for millions of years survived for less than two centuries after human beings invaded its habitat.

Maria Theresa became archduchess of Austria in 1740 on the death of her father, Charles VI. She was only 23. Some neighboring countries opposed her because they didn't feel that a woman should inherit a throne. She fought several wars to prove herself, and became known as one of the best rulers of the 18th century.

In and Out of Fashion

For nearly a decade after the publication of *The Four Seasons,* Vivaldi is absent from the records of the Pietà. The reason appears to be a simple one: the composer was taking advantage of his fame to produce even more operas and to travel extensively. Even with improvements in transportation, travel at that time was difficult. Riding in a horse-drawn coach, Vivaldi probably took an entire day to cover distances that we routinely cover on a modern highway in a single hour or even less. We don't know about all the places that he visited, though it is fairly certain they included Prague (in today's Czech Republic), Munich (Germany), and Vienna (Austria). His trip to Vienna in 1728 was especially important, because he became acquainted with Holy Roman Emperor Charles VI.

Vivaldi wasn't always going from one place to another. He returned to Venice on numerous occasions, primarily to oversee the productions of the new operas that he was continuing to write for his home city. There are records of at least 11 different Vivaldi operas in Venice during this time, four in 1726 alone.

In 1735, Vivaldi again returned to the Pietà. The tone of the contract seems somewhat disrespectful to the man who was prob-

ably the most famous composer living in Europe. It reads, in part, "with no idea of leaving any more as has been his practice in past years."[1]

Since he was now 57, he may also have appreciated the quiet, reflective atmosphere of the Pietà. It would have offered him peace from the harsh demands of touring so often. Another reason could be that by then, his work was starting to fall out of fashion. He may have wanted something secure for his old age, a sort of early form of Social Security.

But for more than two decades, Vivaldi had traveled to the grandest cities of Europe and been hailed as a great violinist and composer. Despite his contract with the Pietà, within two years he was restless again. In 1737 he tried to establish a successful opera season in Ferrara, a town about 75 miles south of Venice. At first all went well. In one of his few surviving letters, Vivaldi wrote to his patron, "I assert your Excellency that one has formed here such a company as, I trust, will not for years to come have been seen on the stage at Ferrara."[2]

Vivaldi's careful preparations were for naught. Late that year, the Cardinal of Ferrara, Tomaso Ruffo, forbade Vivaldi to produce his operas. There were two reasons given: Vivaldi was a priest who didn't conduct masses, and he was allegedly having a scandalous relationship with a singer named Anna Girò.

There had long been rumors about Vivaldi's relationship with Anna, who was considerably younger than the composer. Most people believe that he met her during his first years in Mantua. She appeared in many of his operas during the 1720s. When he began traveling extensively, she and her sister often accompanied him. Even in an era where moral standards may have been a little lax, that was very questionable behavior for a priest.

Vivaldi was horrified by the ban. He sent a long letter to his patron. "It is impossible to give the opera without la Girò," he wrote. "What grieves me most is that His Eminence Ruffo puts a stain on these poor women [Anna and her sister] which the world never gave them. For more than 14 years we have traveled together; we were in many European cities, and everywhere their honesty was admired, and one can say that also in Ferrara. Every week they do their devotions, witnesses can swear to this, as one who is sworn to one's faith should do."[3]

He also explained in some detail why he hadn't said mass. He brought up his chest problem, even claiming that Anna and her sister helped to nurse him during his sufferings. Despite his pleadings, however, the ban remained in force.

Early in 1738, Vivaldi traveled to Amsterdam, home of his publisher. He had been invited there to direct a series of performances.

Even without the Ferrara scandal, Vivaldi's fortunes were on the wane back home. In 1739, Charles de Brosses wrote, "I found to my great astonishment that he [Vivaldi] was not as esteemed as he deserves in this country where all is fashion, where his works have been heard for a long time and the music of the preceding years no longer brings in receipts."[4]

Vivaldi had one last triumph at the Pietà. It was in the spring of 1740, to honor a visit by Prince Frederick Christian, the son of the king of Poland. Vivaldi wrote several compositions for the occasion, and the concert was a great success.

By then, Vivaldi had decided to leave his native city. One theory is that he wanted to get a position in Vienna at the court of Charles VI, a longtime admirer. But Charles died in October 1740, after eating a plate of poisonous mushrooms. For Vivaldi, the timing couldn't have been worse. Charles's successor, the Empress Maria

Theresa, inherited a number of urgent political problems that she had to solve right away. The difficulties of an aging, somewhat out-of-fashion composer would have been of no interest to her.

Vivaldi's final mention in the Pietà records is on August 29, 1740. He sold several concertos for considerably less than his usual fee, which suggests that he was in desperate need of money for his travel preparations. A brief item in a French newspaper noted the publication of six of his cello concertos in December 1740.

After that, he seemed to have vanished. No one knew what had happened to him. Finally, almost two centuries later, in 1938, his burial records were discovered in Vienna's church of St. Stephen. He had died on July 28, 1741, and was buried the same day. The cause of death was listed as an "internal inflammation," which could have meant any one of many medical conditions.

He received the minimum funeral, which consisted of six pall-bearers and six choirboys. One of the young singers was nine-year-old Franz Joseph Haydn, who would become one of the greatest composers of the second half of the 18th century. Vivaldi's gravesite has long since disappeared.

Pincherle notes that Vivaldi "was famous and feted during his lifetime, and his music was performed and plagiarized throughout Europe. But soon after his death, or even a little before, he passed into a state of neglect that seemed final."[5]

With the revival of *The Four Seasons* and renewed interest in his other compositions, Vivaldi's reputation has been restored.

As John Booth says, "Venice and Vivaldi, the two words are closely linked in the mind but Venice is a curiosity, magical but ghostly, a jewelled and fantastic relic, while Vivaldi's music is vibrant, surging with life and energy, as passionate and compelling as when it first echoed in the city of the sea."[6]

Jonathan Swift FYInfo

The author Jonathan Swift was born in Dublin, Ireland, on November 30, 1667. His father had died several months earlier, leaving his widow with a young daughter and infant son and almost no money to support them.

Jonathan Swift

When Jonathan was four, his mother moved to England. Jonathan moved in with his uncle, who sent him to several excellent schools. But he was too rebellious to be a good student.

After an anti-Catholic rebellion in Ireland, Jonathan moved to England in 1689 and spent the next 10 years there, beginning his writing career. In 1695 he was ordained as a minister. He also became involved in politics. After traveling back and forth between England and Ireland, he returned to Ireland for good in 1713, taking a position as dean of St. Patrick's Cathedral in Dublin.

His most famous book was *Gulliver's Travels,* published in 1726. It is about the adventures of Lemuel Gulliver, whose voyages end in unusual circumstances. First he is shipwrecked among Lilliputians, human-like creatures just six inches tall. Then he finds himself among the Brobdingnagians, who are giants.

The book concludes with a voyage to a land where the usual roles of humans and horses are reversed. The horses, called Houyhnhnms (pronounced WHIN-nee-ims), are highly intelligent and cultured. Their servants are savage, stupid human-like creatures called Yahoos.

In 1729 Swift wrote "A Modest Proposal." At that time, Ireland was suffering from two problems: overpopulation and a shortage of food. Swift suggested a solution to both problems. The infant children of poor people could be sold to the wealthy to be used as food. Of course, Swift wasn't serious. He was expressing his anger at what he regarded as the oppression of the Irish people by the ruling English.

Because of a disease of the inner ear, Swift suffered from deafness and vertigo for many years. His health began to decline even more during the 1730s, and he suffered a stroke in 1742, which left him almost helpless. He died in Dublin on October 19, 1745.

Selected Works

Concertos

Vivaldi is generally credited with developing the musical form of the concerto. He wrote more than 650 that featured a variety of instruments, including violin, cello, mandolin, flute, bassoon, recorder and oboe. It is likely that even more may be discovered. The most famous are:

The Four Seasons (part of *Il cimento dell'armonia e dell'inventione*)
L'estro armonico
La stravaganza

Oratorios

Moyses deus Pharaonis
Juditha triumphans

Operas

Vivaldi claimed to have written 94 operas, though only about 50 have been discovered. Performances of Vivaldi operas are very rare.

Sacred Music

Gloria in D
Magnificat
Kyrie
Credo

Chronology

1678 Born on March 4 in Venice, Italy
1693 Begins training to become a priest
1703 Ordained as priest; appointed as violin teacher at the Pietà
1705 First musical composition, a collection of trio sonatas, is published
1709 Fired from position at the Pietà
1711 Rehired at the Pietà; *L'estro armonico* is published
1713 Composes first opera, *Ottone in villa*
1716 Composes oratorio *Juditha Triumphans*
1718 Moves to Mantua; probably meets Anna Girò
1723 Returns to Venice
1724 Plays violin for Pope Innocent XIII
1725 Publishes *The Four Seasons*
1728 Travels to Vienna, Austria, and meets Emperor Charles VI
1735 Reappointed at the Pietà
1737 Denied permission to stage operas in Ferrara
1738 Travels to Amsterdam, The Netherlands
1740 Leaves for Vienna
1741 Dies and is buried in Vienna on July 28
.....
1920s Some of Vivaldi's music found in a library in Turin
1939 His music performed in public for the first time in nearly 200 years
1950 *The Four Seasons* is republished
1990 Nigel Kennedy's *Four Seasons* becomes the most popular Vivaldi recording in history

Timeline in History

1620 Pilgrims land at Plymouth Rock in Massachusetts.

1638 King Louis XIV of France is born.

1659 Composer Henry Purcell is born.

1672 Czar Peter the Great of Russia is born.

1676 Dutch scientist Anton van Leeuwenhoek uses microscope to observe tiny living organisms in pondwater.

1678 Elena Lucrezia Cornaro Piscopia becomes first woman to receive Ph.D. (doctor of philosophy) degree.

1680 Flightless bird dodo becomes extinct.

1682 La Salle claims Louisiana Territory for France.

1683 First coffee houses appear in Vienna, Austria.

1685 Composers George Frideric Handel, Johann Sebastian Bach, and Domenico Scarlatti are born.

1706 American statesman and inventor Benjamin Franklin is born.

1709 Italian instrument maker Bartolomeo Cristofori invents the piano.

1715 King Louis XIV of France dies and his great-grandson becomes King Louis XV.

1716 Venice wins war with Turkey regarding possession of the island of Corfu.

1719 Daniel Defoe publishes *Robinson Crusoe*.

1726 Jonathan Swift publishes *Gulliver's Travels*.

1732 George Washington is born.

1735 Paul Revere is born.

1737 Italian violin maker Antonio Stradivari dies.

1741 Handel composes his oratorio *Messiah*.

1750 Composer Johann Sebastian Bach dies.

1756 Composer Wolfgang Amadeus Mozart is born.

1770 Composer Ludwig van Beethoven is born.

Chapter Notes

Chapter 1   Rediscovering a Forgotten Composer

1. Marc Pincherle, *Vivaldi: Genius of the Baroque,* translated by Christopher Hatch (London: Victor Gollancz Ltd., 1958), p. 14.

2. H. C. Robbins Landon, *Vivaldi: Voice of the Baroque* (New York: Thames and Hudson, 1993), p. 7.

Chapter 3   The Pietà

1. Michael Talbot, *Vivaldi* (New York: Schirmer Books, 1993), p. 31.

2. Karl Heller, *Antonio Vivaldi: The Red Priest of Venice,* translated by David Marinelli (Portland, Oreg.: Amadeus Press, 1997), p. 43.

3. John Booth, *The Illustrated Lives of the Great Composers: Vivaldi* (London: Omnibus Press, 1989), pp. 24, 26.

Chapter 4   A Burst of Creative Energy

1. Walter Kolneder, *Antonio Vivaldi: His Life and Works,* translated by Bill Hopkins (Berkeley, Calif.: University of California Press, 1970), p. 11.

2. H. C. Robbins Landon, *Vivaldi: Voice of the Baroque* (New York: Thames and Hudson, 1993), p. 36.

3. John Booth, *The Illustrated Lives of the Great Composers: Vivaldi* (London: Omnibus Press, 1989), p. 122.

4. Michael Talbot, *Vivaldi* (New York: Schirmer Books, 1993), p. 43.

5. Booth, p. 59.

Chapter 5   The Four Seasons

1. H. C. Robbins Landon, *Vivaldi: Voice of the Baroque* (New York: Thames and Hudson, 1993), p. 67.

Chapter 6   In and Out of Fashion

1. Marc Pincherle, *Vivaldi: Genius of the Baroque,* translated by Christopher Hatch (London: Victor Gollancz Ltd., 1958), p. 49.

2. H. C. Robbins Landon, *Vivaldi: Voice of the Baroque* (New York: Thames and Hudson, 1993), p. 131.

3. Ibid., p. 148.

4. John Booth, *The Illustrated Lives of the Great Composers: Vivaldi* (London: Omnibus Press, 1989), p. 107.

5. Pincherle, p. 13.

6. Booth, p. 128.

For Further Reading

For Young Adults

Anderson, M. T. *Handel: Who Knew What He Liked*. Cambridge, Mass.: Candlewick Press, 2001.

Vernon, Roland. *Introducing Bach*. Parsippany, N.J.: Silver Burdett Press, 1996.

————. *Introducing Vivaldi*. Parsippany, N.J.: Silver Burdett Press, 1997.

Vivaldi, Antonio. *The Four Seasons* (includes compact disc). Boston: Bulfinch Press, 1999.

Works Consulted

Booth, John. *The Illustrated Lives of the Great Composers: Vivaldi*. London: Omnibus Press, 1989.

Heller, Karl. *Antonio Vivaldi: The Red Priest of Venice*. Translated by David Marinelli. Portland, Oreg.: Amadeus Press, 1997.

Kolneder, Walter. *Antonio Vivaldi: His Life and Works*. Translated by Bill Hopkins. Berkeley, Calif.: University of California Press, 1970.

Pincherle, Marc. *Vivaldi: Genius of the Baroque*. Translated by Christopher Hatch. London: Victor Gollancz Ltd., 1958.

Robbins Landon, H. C. *Vivaldi: Voice of the Baroque*. New York: Thames and Hudson, 1993.

Talbot, Michael. *Vivaldi*. New York: Schirmer Books, 1993.

Internet Addresses

Antonio Vivaldi
http://www.antonio-vivaldi.org/
http://www.classical.net/music/comp.lst/vivaldi.html
http://www.classicalarchives.com/vivaldi.html
FYI: Two Great Baroque Masters
http://www.jsbach.org/
http://www.classical.net/music/comp.lst/bachjs.html

http://www.GFHandel.org
http://www.amarcordes.ch/compositeurs/haendel_grove.htm
FYI: The City of Flooded Streets
http://www.ambrit-rome.com/clasproj/venice/vhistory.htm
http://www.doge.it
FYI: The World's Most Famous Violins
http://www.physics.uoguelph.ca/summer/scor/articles/scor166.htm
http://www.freep.com/entertainment/music/ds029_20021229.htm
FYI: The Sun King
http://www.royalty.nu/Europe/France/LouisXIV.html
http://www.bcpl.net/-cbladey/loo.html
FYI: The Dodo
http://www.usatoday.com/news/science/biology/2002-02-28-dodo.htm
http://www.answersingenesis.org/docs/1172.asp
http://news.nationalgeographic.com/news/2002/02/0227_0228_dodo.html
FYI: Jonathan Swift
http://www.incwell.com/Biographies/Swift.html
http://www.kirjasto.sci.fi/jswift.htm

Index